School-Ministers

Shaping a New Generation of Church Leaders

Lallie Godfrey

Schools' Team Leader,
Diocese of Chelmsford Education Department

Andy Griffiths

Coordinator of Training for New Ministers,
Diocese of Chelmsford

GROVE BOOKS LIMITED
RIDLEY HALL RD CAMBRIDGE CB3 9HU

Contents

Anglican Association of Directors of Education

First Impression January 2020
ISSN 2041-0964
ISBN 978 1 78827 109 7

Preface

> Chris, have you met Bridgette? Ah, Alan, great you're here—have you met Chris and Bridgette?—you all work in the *same* diocese.

I have a vivid memory of making such introductions to people at a national day conference we organized not long after the publication of a landmark report on church schools, *The Way Ahead*, in 2001. Our purpose was to explore how those preparing for ordained ministry could also be prepared for schools ministry. So we brought together leaders of theological colleges and courses, directors of ordinands and directors of education. Rowan Williams—then Archbishop of Wales—spoke with passion about the vital importance of Christian ministry in schools, urging joined-up thinking in training provision.

Some clearly immediately got it. A couple of principals from very different traditions, both formerly parish priests, described serious work their colleges did. Others struggled. 'We don't do training, we do formation,' declared one, rather loftily. 'Our problem is there's too much to do already, and we work in different departments,' observed others.

A decade later we had another go. A working group was convened—how we Anglicans love these! Since schools have been an integral part of the Church of England for over 200 years, surely something about them should be taught *before* ordination, followed by practical training *after* ordination. About 722,000 attend Sunday worship across about 12,600 parishes (2017 stats). Meanwhile, 1,000,000 pupils attend about 4,700 church schools. The chances of ministers working with one at some stage are high, whilst developing a ministry with some sort of school is almost universal in parish ministry.

So we suggested a pilot project be run for the post-ordination phase of ministry (curacy). Chelmsford, a large and very diverse diocese, agreed. Hence this booklet, written five years into the programme. Schools welcome involvement, whilst ministers speak warmly of the experience and some attest to it having a transformational influence on them. The practicalities of schemes will differ in other contexts—but getting on with *something* in a joined-up way is vital to the formation and training of our clergy if they are to be effective.

Tim Elbourne
Director of Education
Diocese of Chelmsford

1 Introduction: Shaping Ministers

What shape is your minister? We do not mean long and thin or short and round—but has your minister been shaped into the kind of human being God has in mind? We are not to be the same as each other—God will not ask Andy why he was not Lallie, but God might ask him why he was not fully Andy. But within their diversity, ministers are supposed to *be* a certain sort of person, *know* certain things and *be able to do* certain things. We refer to these ways of being, knowing and ability to do as *dispositions, understandings* and *skills*.

This booklet is arguing that schools are the missing link in ensuring ministers end up the right shape. It has two audiences in mind. First, it aims to speak to ministers and those who train them, especially in training pre-ordination (known as IME1) and training immediately after ordination (known as IME2, during curacy). Although we are both Anglicans, we hope that what we write will be applicable to ministers and their trainers in all sorts of denominational settings. By the time these people have read this booklet, we hope they will be convinced that involvement in schools is a key part of the shaping of ministers, and have some practical ideas about how this might be brought about.

The second audience in our minds is school leaders. We hope to enlist them in the task of shaping ministers, whilst demonstrating that the ministers formed in this way will make a vital contribution to schools in future. We are trying to convince you that schools have a role in ministerial formation and that schools have a gap within them which exactly fits this kind of school-shaped minister.

Because churches have an understanding that their ministers will be a certain shape, chapter two below gives an overview of the kind of formational criteria presently in use, and a brief historical sketch indicating how we have arrived at our models of how these criteria are to be met. We realize parts of this chapter are not easy reading—seventeenth-century bishops may not be your thing—but we hope to show that the three historic strands in ministerial formation have a lot in common with three present-day theories of education. Chapter three considers the claim that involvement in schools should be seen as part of the mechanism of shaping ministers. Chapter four details a project in the Diocese of Chelmsford which enables school placements for curates. Chapters five and six then outline the impact of school involvement on ministers, both short and long term, and the impact on schools of school-shaped ministers.

Shaping Ministers—the Present Model

2

There is something missing in theological education. In our next chapter, we will be suggesting what the missing link is, but first we need to outline the three strands through which ministers are presently shaped.

All professions shape their professionals.[1] It might almost be said that the absence of this shaping, sometimes called professional formation, means that a way of life is not really a profession. In this sense, professions are institutions. Hugh Heclo pictures a time portal in a staff room (or its equivalent) through which past professionals step to ask, 'What have you done with what we bequeathed you?' and future professionals step back to ask, 'Why didn't you pass on to us in better order the institutions you received?'[2]

Churches are no exception. Indeed, much of the thrust towards creating theological colleges to train priests in the Victorian age was a conscious attempt to mimic other professions and so ensure a professional identity for the clergy.[3] Ministers' *dispositions, understanding* and *skills* are to be shaped. The section that follows explains these three terms and talks about the way the shaping is expected to take place, through such elements as habit-forming, supervision, formal instruction, mentoring and peer support. We also seek to show how this shaping bears much in common with the training of teachers and school leaders, and indeed with successive Secretary of States' views of how education should proceed for children.

Dispositions: Jesus, Jeremy Taylor and Schools of Character

How do the four gospels represent the way that Jesus taught others? There is little formal education—though there are some long private discourses and public sermons—and little skills training—the closest thing we can find is telling the disciples that a certain kind of evil spirit only comes out with prayer. Rather, we can see storytelling, modelling, establishing community, action-reflection models with an observation, action and report-back cycle (see, for example, Luke 10), questioning, and other activities.

Jesus is interested in changing *who we are*, not just *what we know* or *what we can do*. This is all best recorded in the work of Sylvia Collinson. Collinson argues that Jesus' mix is surprisingly congruent with some models of education today. We are moving from a sort of learning that focuses on what she calls 'the schooling model' of formal education alone, to one in which modelling, questioning, storytelling and communal action-reflection are once again accepted as valid, with outcomes that are about *being*, not just *knowing* or *ability to do* as legitimate goals.[4]

Those who train ministers tend to use the word 'disposition.' Dispositions are:

> Habits and values related to character development...discerned relationally and developed through a combination of learning, experience, reflection and prayer.[5]
>
> The soul's characteristic response to the call of God and the cries of others.[6]

This way of understanding education should not be unfamiliar to those in schools, for a line can be drawn:

- *from* much recent theology, which speaks of '*habitus*,'[7] 'virtue ethics,'[8] and 'shaping' (theologian David Ford speaks of 'everyday disciplines that change our desires little by little,' especially the discipline of forgetting ourselves in worship)[9]
- *via* the work of Frances Ward, former Dean of St Edmundsbury [10]
- *to* Nicky Morgan, Secretary of State for Education 2014–2016, and her advocacy of what she called 'Schools of Character.'[11]

Nor is this accidental—Ward acknowledges Ford's work, whilst Morgan acknowledges Ward's and McIntyre's. But where did Ford's thinking come from? He is explicitly drawing on the generation of English theologians from the time of Charles II, including Jeremy Taylor, the major Anglican theologian of the seventeenth century.[12]

Taylor held that:

> The only learning that signifies [really matters] is learning that makes us better; anything else is but the skinning of an old sore...It is not the wit of the man, but the spirit of the man, not so much the head as the heart, that learns the divine philosophy.[13]

He believed that what we need is, 'a deliciousness that makes us love the things of God,' a quality in us which responds appropriately to the attractiveness of God. The alternative (seeking learning without a change of character—'knowing more' and 'doing more' without 'being') is mere 'prettiness.'

We might say that there is a circular effect:

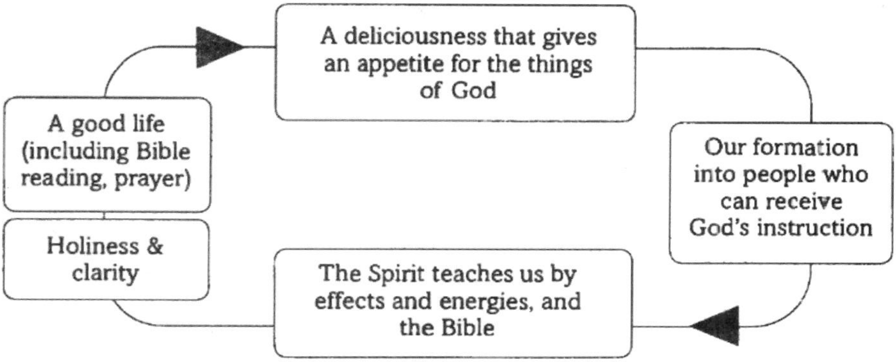

Settled habits transform us, so that we develop what might be called a second nature—a new way of behaving and of seeing the world, which has become natural to us and is resilient in a way that mere learned behaviour is not.[14]

And so it should come as no surprise that when the Church of England provides formational criteria that relate to dispositions (the first list below), there is a structural similarity with Morgan's lists (the second list). Dispositions are back in education, for schools and ministers alike.

Ordained ministers...

- Value breadth and diversity
- Respect others and demonstrate honesty and empathy (and so on for several pages).

By the end of IME2 [the second phase of their ministerial formation, around three years after ordination] they will show all the above, and

- Show insight, resilience, maturity and integrity
- Model servant leadership after the example of Christ...'[15]

A 'golden child' is...

- A person who tries their best
- Responsible, a good decision-maker, knowing right from wrong
- A good friend
- Confident about themselves
- Resilient
- Ambitious
- Safe

By Year 6 a child will be all of the above, and also

- Know their academic strengths
- Know their talents[16]

Understanding: the University Model and Addressing the Knowledge Deficit

In his time as Secretary of State for Education (2010–2014), Michael Gove came to believe that education had lost its necessary function of prioritizing 'knowledge as well as skills' and sought to address the 'knowledge deficit' of the disadvantaged.[17]

In so doing he was explicitly drawing on the work of Ed Hirsch and others, who in turn were following a tradition of education that seeks to privilege understanding alongside, and even ahead of, the dispositions. The most coherent case for this tradition is made by John Henry Newman in his *The Idea of a University*, first published in 1852. For Newman, the aim 'is simply the cultivation of the intellect, as such, and its object is nothing more or less than intellectual exercise.'[18] As David H Kelsey points out, intellectual excellence is to Newman what moral excellence is in ancient Greece (*paideia*), and this is why understanding is pursued not for some functional goal, but for its own sake.[19]

Influenced by Newman and others, the university model of formation came to dominate in the first years of the twentieth century, in school and theological education alike, with thinkers such as D T Howard:

> I have always been interested in that question, as to the value of emotional states, and the conclusion to which I have come is that they have absolutely no value at all, but represent an insignificant defect in human nature.[20]

Theological educators today are not disciples of Howard, or indeed Gove. However, they are concerned to ensure that a professional formation values knowledge and understanding for their own sake, and not only for their utility for some other purpose.

Skills: the Oslo Model and the Skills-based Curriculum

Skills-based curriculums were very much in the zeitgeist of the 1990s, and Kenneth Baker, now Lord Baker of Dorking, who was Secretary of State for Education in that era and influenced the creation of the National Curriculum, has continued to argue for a more skills-based approach to education than that espoused by his successors.[21] Whilst these trends were affecting the Ministry of Education, long consultations at the World Council of Churches meeting in Oslo in 1996 also led the Council to propose a skills-based curriculum focused on six competences, held in rough balance, which were identified as pastoral, missionary, ecumenical, theological, spiritual and leadership.

Though the theological curriculum, like the school curriculum, is now seldom structured in this way, educators in both realms still attempt to develop skills, often putting to the fore reflective practice with a teacher/supervisor (churches often call them training incumbents) and supportive peers.[22] In this respect at least, ministers who have been teachers have clear advantages. Howard Worsley notes:

> In my twenty years as a theological educator in Anglican residential colleges...those who come forward to train for ordained ministry from being school teachers, are often in a strong place...and the transferable skills from schools are enormously useful for ordained ministry. These skills include: multi-tasking, strong organization, good communication, thinking on one's feet, collaboration, creativity and subject specialism.[23]

To summarize this overview, ministers' *dispositions*, *understanding* and *skills* are to be shaped. This shaping is to be done in an accountable way, with specific criteria which need to be evidenced by the developing ministers before they can pass on to the next stage of their ministries. This shaping is achieved by a combination of habit-forming, spiritual disciplines, supervision by a reflective practitioner, formal instruction, mentoring, action learning, e-learning and peer support and is, in principle, not unlike the education of children or school leaders. While successive Secretaries of State have championed one or other of character, knowledge and skills, churches have tended to see the three in balance.

Now, it could be said that the place of schools in ministerial education is to teach skills. But in fact, none of the Church of England's skills criteria make any mention of schools. There are associated dispositions ('committed to education, [and to] promoting good practice both inside and outside the church') and understandings ('understand the importance of the Church of England's engagement with schools, for the common good and for the mission and ministry of the church'), but no skills. When we argue that school involvement is the missing link in ministerial education, we mean something much more profound than 'Ministers need skills to work in schools.' We mean, 'Without involvement with schools, ministers will neither *be who they should be* nor *understand what they should understand*.' Our next chapter will consider this in greater depth.

3 Why Schools Need to be Involved in Shaping Ministers

The main point of this chapter is that Jesus makes interaction with children central, and he insists on seeing the behaviour of disciples with children as an indicator of their closeness to the kingdom of heaven. When we assert that schools shaping ministers is the missing link, we mean that when classic models of ministerial formation miss out these two key aspects of his teaching, we all miss out on Jesus' intentions.

The Centrality of Children

Marcia Bunge claims that the marginalization of children in some recent theological thought is linked to the dehumanization of children,[24] which has made widespread abuse in religious settings possible.[25] But this marginalization is not inherent or original in the Christian tradition. On the contrary, in Mark 9, Jesus took a child, put the child in the midst of his disciples and said, 'Whoever receives such a child in my name, receives me' (Mark 9.37). And so, according to the World Council of Churches (WCC):

> Churches from the very beginning of Christianity have understood themselves as agents and advocates of children, reflecting their crucial role in the processes of transformation which belong to the essence of becoming disciples of Jesus Christ and witnessing for the kingdom of God.[26]

Unlike our present consumerist society, Jesus does not see a child as a pseudo-adult.[27] On the contrary, 'It is not the child's transformation to adulthood, but the adults' transformation to childhood [that] determines Jesus' words about the child.'[28] So paying attention to children should be elevated as a means of ministerial shaping to go alongside habit-forming, spiritual disciplines, supervision by a reflective practitioner, formal instruction, action learning and peer support.

The Anglican poet, Thomas Traherne, suggests that a lack of playfulness will lead to a lack of learning—'To be Good, to be Holy, to be Righteous, is freely to Delight in Excellent Actions with a Delight that Grown Men have lost.'[29] Worship is a 'sacred game,' and to have forgotten how to play is to have forgotten how to worship—to be deprived of a chance to 'be taken out of ourselves and participate in the fullness of God.'[30] For George Monbiot, the playfulness of children is also crucial in teaching adults to 'go feral,' 'rewild,' and replace our 'silent spring' with 'the hope of a raucous summer, in which, in some parts of the world at least, destructive processes are thrown into reverse.'[31] Nor will it do to take 'having a child in the midst' as some sort of metaphor for faith or humility, or to take children/little ones as a symbol of the least powerful in society. An absence of attention to real, literal children will render the shaping of a Christian leader inadequate—not only in terms of school skills but for their whole formation.

Behaviour with Children as a Key Indicator that Shaping has been Successful

How children are treated indicates not only whether curates are school-shaped but also whether they are minister-shaped. Matthew 18 insists on this, extending the point that 'Whoever welcomes one such child in my name welcomes me' both negatively—to be a stumbling block for a child is to invite a fate worse than having a millstone attached to your neck and being drowned—and positively—it is the Father's will that not one of these little ones be lost. Along the way is the intriguing verse that says that 'The angels of these little [children] continually see the face of my Father in heaven' (v 10). This seems to be less a doctrinal point about guardian angels than a warning to the disciples that their conduct with children is being observed and evaluated. We might say that the formation assessments of heaven pay special attention to how ministers relate to children. Only after these ground rules have been laid down does Matthew 18 go on to speak of the foundation of the church (one of only two occasions in the gospels when the word 'church' is used). This is serious: a new minister who 'shhh-es' children in church because they are distracting worshippers would need to work hard to convince us that he or she is ready to progress to the next stage of ministry—although, to quote Paul Goodliff, 'I am not saying that as children grow they should not be taught to moderate their innate capacity for chaos.'[32]

It would be tedious to list every formation criterion for new ministers and add: 'This will, in part, be formed through observing children, and will, in part, be evidenced in relation to children.' However, we contend that this would be possible. (For example: 'Incumbents replenish their leadership through a life of disciplined study…this will, in part, be formed through observing children, and will, in part, be evidenced in relation to children.') The point is that curacy and its equivalents are simply going to be inadequate if schools are not part of it—and not only because the new ministers will not be school-shaped, but also because they will not be properly shaped in the other ways that the church demands.

Child Theology

This way of insisting on the presence of children chimes well with a significant movement in theology known as the Child Theology (CT) Movement. CT is not merely theologizing about how we treat children; it sees itself as a fully valid contextual theology alongside black theology, deaf theology, liberation theology, feminist theologies and others.[33] It would be as wrong to say that Child Theology has nothing to say about ministerial formation as it would be wrong to say that black theology has nothing to say about the atonement. As the table below suggests, all theological subjects are critiqued, and engaged by, contextual theologies.

Theological subject	Traditional name	How critiqued by Child Theology
Who Jesus is	Christology	Jesus says that to receive a child is to receive him, and to receive him is to receive the one that sent him
What the church is	ecclesiology	A child is the prophetic sign of the church[34]
How the church is led	theology of leadership	The answer to the question 'which of these leaders is the greatest?' is to put a child in the midst
What will happen at the end of the age	eschatology	'A little child shall lead them,' and the child of Matthew 18 is already a sign of the new creation[35]

Moreover, in the call to identify with the child, CT goes significantly beyond other anti-patriarchal contextual theologies:

> With respect to those of another gender, ethnicity, race or religious commitment, the claim to identification [is] bogus, despite our common humanity, the possibility of empathy and the potential of creative imagination...but...we have all been children and have memories of experiencing childhood.[36]

Though the movement is still developing, it already has a classic work of introduction.[37]

Well-being

One last point about the role of schools in shaping ministers is that it would be rash to ignore the contribution that schools make towards well-being. Take, for example, the recent report published by the Church of England Education Office on 'Mental Health and Well-being.'[38] This begins by quoting the philosopher Nicholas Wolterstorff's suggestion that the ultimate goal for Christian educators should be to seek *shalom*—a biblical vision of what God wants for humans which can be defined as flourishing in the enjoyment of relationships—with self, others, creation and with God. It goes on to consider the importance of mental health and well-being as part of a holistic vision for education, where equipping young people to navigate and enjoy good relationships is a key factor in supporting their mental health and well-being, where justice is valued and injustice challenged. In the words of the report:

> ...the new Statutory Inspection of Anglican and Methodist Schools (SIAMS) framework calls for pupils to develop courageous advocacy and to see themselves as agents of change, making the world we live in a better place for everyone.

Now, reading this report would in itself contribute to a better understanding of human flourishing for new ministers—and we do indeed recommend it. But it would be far more powerful for a new minister to spend time being part of a school community that was flourishing in this way and manifesting *shalom*, justice and change for the better. This would make a difference to the minister's own well-being. Involvement with school would not only make them school-shaped, it would make them *shalom*-shaped.

Category	**Refers to...**	**Classic means of ministerial formation**	**Parallel with educational agenda**[39]	**School-based means of ministerial formation**
Dispositions	...being	Habit-forming, social action, spirituality, worship, mentors	Nicky Morgan's 'schools of character'	Becoming childlike, playfulness, rewilding, immersion in community of *shalom*
Understandings	...knowing	Formal learning, e-learning, action learning, group learning	Michael Gove's 'knowledge curriculum'	Observing child in the midst, learning with/ from children, letting CT critique theology
Skills	...ability to do	Reflective practice with a supervisor, peer support	Kenneth Baker's 'skills-based curriculum'	Skills practice in schools

Curates' School Placements

The shaping of ministers for and through schools is not common practice across dioceses and a recent survey of curates elicited comments such as:

- 'You don't get any training to do with what you do in schools.'
- 'I don't think I got anything in training.'
- 'Training? Nothing, no...we must have done some? But nothing kind of practical, we must have talked about it probably...it hasn't made much of an impression (laughs).'
- 'I'd say there's no support in current training opportunities...well maybe if I went and looked for it...but certainly there's nothing that is offered to me.'[40]

The Diocese of Chelmsford recognized a need and so the Diocesan Director of Education, together with the Mission and Ministry Department, piloted the Curate School Placement programme in 2014. Currently the programme is mandatory for all those training to be incumbents and voluntary for all other second-year curates. However, each year several self-supporting curates have taken part in the programme and found the experience beneficial.

Expectations

Before the placement we asked schools:

- What support do you currently receive from your local/church incumbent?
- What does the school do either with, or in, the local church?
- If your incumbent could give one hour per week to your school, what would you like her or him to do?
- What do you think a school-shaped vicar would look like?

The answers to the first two questions tended to be similar, with reference to being a governor, leading collective worship and using the school for key Christian festivals and for Religious Education (RE).

However, the final two questions were more illuminating. As far as the majority of head teachers were concerned, collective worship and being a governor were not as high a priority as first thought. Examples given for what schools would like if they could have one hour per week included statements such as:

- 'Be visible to the community, like a chaplain; visit the children at play and the staff at coffee; and lead something pastoral / worshipful which involves blessing.'
- 'Presence in playground and staff room at break times or lunchtime; time with HT to share whatever needs sharing and to be there for support / guidance.'
- 'Work in classes answering difficult questions!'
- 'Work with the worship committee and hold a Bible / prayer club for the children.'

This made us wonder whether schools make it clear to clergy what type of support they actually want from them. Indeed, one incumbent was surprised to note that what the school had identified as something that they would like was not what he had been asked to do by a senior leader, yet he would have relished the opportunity to do what they were wanting. Therefore, it was important that in the Curate School Placement programme curates were not limited to certain activities and indeed, where possible, actively discouraged from undertaking activities such as collective worship.

The majority of responses to what a school-shaped vicar would look like focused on relationships with children and staff, and the need for all to be supported. The quotations below emphasize the fact the head teachers really understood the value that having a minister in their midst could add:

- 'They are child centred...can get down to the children's level in terms of delivery.'
- 'They can act as a go-between for the older members of the congregation who have set views.'
- 'They are fun and can have a laugh with the staff—they are human!'
- 'Someone who supported the ethos of the school and its commitment to educating about all religions...Easily contactable and accessible...Someone who lived and breathed hands-on Christianity.'

- 'They recognize that our school is a village school as well as a church school...They have time for all staff...Ready to work together to try new ideas.'
- 'Someone able to lead children into real sensitive experiences of worship and faith—making the spiritual journey an important thing, not trivializing it.'
- 'They believe in the essential wonder and goodness of everyone. Shape? Rounded!'

Prior to the placement, curates are asked to give an outline of their own personal educational experience. Curates who have worked in education are often unsure whether they will gain anything at all from a placement but are encouraged to undertake it and note how relationships change once the person enters the school wearing a dog collar. For those who have not been in a school since they themselves were pupils, it may feel a daunting challenge. However, support and guidance are given, reminding the curates that the schools themselves will ensure that they are both welcomed and supported throughout the placement.

> I went into the school placement thinking I have seen all this before and to be honest...I was wondering if this was a good use of my time. Having completed the placement I am so grateful it is in the curacy programme. It made me realize and see for myself the wonderful mission opportunity we have in our church schools.

Process

The placement schools are selected based on the travel distance for curates but, where possible, not within their training parish, so that the experience does not conflict with any support they are already offering.

Following the matching process, an initial session is held with the curates who will undertake the placement, at which the Diocese of Chelmsford *Curate School Placement Handbook* is discussed in depth. Curates and head teachers who have previously been a part of the process are invited along to share experiences and to answer questions.

In brief, curates undertaking the school placement will:

- Have an initial meeting with the head teacher of the school
- Undertake a four-day placement in the school, involving themselves in a variety of activities (greater detail is given later in the chapter)
- Complete a reflective journal on their experience

Following completion of the school placements, a final session is held with the curates where their experiences are shared and there is the opportunity to discuss the impact that this will have on their own future ministry in school.

Within the handbook for curate placements, guidance is given both to the curates and the schools on the expectations of the placements. The following suggestions are given as an aid:

- *Classroom observations:* Different year groups, shadowing a single class for a whole day, specific lessons, for example RE
- *Collective worship:* Observation
- *Informal observations:* Break times
- *Pupil interactions:* School council; pupil groups
- *Governance: eg* meeting chair of governors; governing body meetings and committees; foundation governors
- *Chaplaincy:* (if applicable)
- *Discussion with school staff: eg* senior leadership team; RE co-ordinator; collective worship co-ordinator; SENCO; admin staff; teaching assistants; support staff
- *Meeting local clergy*
- *Pre- and after-school clubs*
- *Parents and PTA:* before and after school on playground, alongside volunteers
- *Documentation: eg* school profile; reports (Ofsted / SIAMS); minutes; policies

Reflection

During and after the school placement, curates are asked to keep a reflective journal. These reflections are used as a basis for the discussions at the final Curate School Placement session where the curates are encouraged to consider the impact that the placement will have on their own personal ministry with schools in the future—in many ways the first shoots of school-shaped ministers start here, which will be addressed in greater depth in the following chapters.

However, not every experience was positive.

- 'What was referred to as worship was not worship in any way, nor did it seem planned. I was asked to speak in an assembly at 30 seconds' notice and discovered this was a common experience for staff.'

- 'There was a lot of talk of Christian values, but little or no mention of the story of Jesus.'
- 'There was less Christian distinctiveness in this church school than in the community school I usually visit—the standard of RE was embarrassing.'

A small number of schools were not prepared for the curate on arrival; in some there was too little time for curates to discuss their reflections with the leaders in the school, or the placements took place during a special week like Easter which meant that the curates did not get to experience the normal provision for the children and staff. Ever since, we have written in advance to local incumbents, giving them a right to object to the process if they wish; no one has ever done so.

Whilst such issues cannot totally be avoided, it is essential to acknowledge them and make efforts to ensure that all are aware of the aims of the school placement. The expectations of the school are now included in the *Curate School Placement Handbook* given to head teachers. In addition, discussions now take place prior to the placement, between the education team leader, head teacher and curates, whilst curates are allocated a named education adviser (linked to the school) who is their point of contact should they need advice or support during the placement. In this way, some of the pitfalls can be avoided and the placement itself will, it is hoped, be the start of the shaping of ministers who will have reflected and subsequently developed their own practice. The intention is that this will ultimately bring a mutually supportive presence into schools for the good of all.

The Impact on Ministers

5

Now we can focus on the outcomes of the placement for the curates, immediately after the placement and in the longer term, once licensed. It is also relevant to reflect on the effect of the curate placement on the subsequent partnership between the school and the supervising incumbent. Evidence of the initial impact of the school placement is gathered through the curates' personal reflective journals, as well as through the final session of the programme, where curates discuss their experience during the school placement and how it has changed their likely future ministry.

Initial Responses

Whilst the curates will have had varied experiences during their placements, generally there are five key themes that have shaped them.

Pressures on Those in Schools

Most often mentioned in the reflective journals is *the pressures on those in schools,* both children and staff, a frequent conclusion reached being that, as a minister, there is a unique opportunity to be the listening ear in a school to whom both children and staff feel safe to talk:

> Today I went home feeling rather exhausted after an emotionally draining day and pondering the many needs of children in school, particularly those who need the extra care and support. Part of the role of the church working alongside school includes being a presence and meeting people where they are...offering a listening ear and support, especially in times of need.

How Willing Children are to Talk and Share with Others

There is also a raised awareness of *how willing children are to talk and share with others,* curates realizing the opportunities that working and being with the children could offer them in their ministry:

> What I found was, in a sense, the same difference as when I first went around the supermarket with my collar on: it somehow gave people the permission they needed to ask questions or bring up discussions that they might not otherwise.

Spirituality

One of our aims was that curates would be able to reflect on *spirituality,* their own and that of children. Nye's report found that, of a large number of clergy interviewed, '*Only one interviewee referred to the way they carried out their church school roles as being in line with their view of children's spirituality.*'[41] Yet for some Chelmsford curates there has been a surprising re-engagement with the child-like nature of their own spirituality:

- 'I realized I've spent so much of my life having to grow up—even in the discernment process—and now I'm looking for ways to become a child again.'
- 'There is a playful, liminal zone, without which ministers become predictable preservers of the *status quo.* I know of no way to get into this zone more effectively than playing games with children.'
- 'I had apparent need to have a role, to make a difference, to rise to a challenge but here was being shown another way of being, which chimed with other things going on in my journey with God…I am programmed to 'do for,' or 'be for' people and here my place was not so much to do but to be, not to shape, organize, lead,…but to deal with the 'givenness' of each moment…My presence was more passive, more contemplative, more mindful. It correlated, perhaps, more closely with Jesus' Nazareth years, the ones we don't hear about, in which he simply abides, he embodies God *with* us. Maybe God was saying, "Shut up, be still, be quiet, watch."'

As Worsley points out, the spirituality of adults is often aided by 'stooping' to be with children, as pilgrims need to do at the entrance of the Church of the Nativity.[42]

For one curate, there was even a surprisingly playful reimagining of a child-like role:

- 'I sat with them, on their little tables and their little seats, and cross-legged on the floor. In this persona, I did much of the work of a teaching assistant. The difference was that I fulfilled this function as a child—with a degree of identification…I wonder if it is the playfulness of role fluidity that [enables] the "all things to all people" element of primary school chaplaincy?…The specifically ministerial nature of chaplaincy in this context is to be with children, as a child, and so to stand with them together at the gates of the kingdom of heaven.'

Rethinking Church Life

There is also evidence of how exposure to school life has helped curates *rethink church life.* For example:

- 'Working in schools might challenge us about what we are doing on Sunday morning. I was particularly struck by the children's willingness to engage with the issues raised in assembly and their genuine conversations when told to talk to their neighbours. This is in contrast to the sense of asking the impossible when I try to elicit responses from the pulpit in church!'
- 'School has a culture which sits in contrast with a more consumer culture in church, where it can sometimes feel like people (adults more than children but both included) are waiting for a worship experience / performance to be presented to them. I am not naive enough to think that schools and their children aren't like this too, at times, but it points once again to one of the reasons Jesus calls us to be like the little children—responsive, open, keen to learn (especially at this age!) and also makes us ask question about how we engage adults, children and people with different learning styles in our churches, remembering they are, amongst other things, also places of learning and community.'
- 'It made me aware of how important / valuable presence in a school is to staff, in particular the head teacher, as what we have in common is the loneliness of the role. You could have more presence talking to parents / governors at the school than on several Sundays.'

Church / School Links

Ways of strengthening *church/school links* are often mentioned. The reality that, in many parishes, the church congregation is both ageing and dwindling is often noted. In the Diocese of Chelmsford (2019) it was estimated that 4,400 children attend a church service on a Sunday. There are 139 church schools in the diocese and every school day, each of the 30,000 children in church schools attend a formal act of worship. If a child was to experience the same level of content in church, they would have to attend church every Sunday, without missing, for 26 years. We have no records of the 750,000 children in other educational settings. This shows the huge potential for ministry in educational settings. However, following the school placements, many curates reflect on the fact that ministry can take place wherever there are people and that, by being a strong and physical presence in a school, they as ministers will be able to undertake their calling for the benefit of the community within which they work:

- 'I realized that we have very different approaches to the mission of the local church in the school. [The vicar] said there were barriers to his involvement in the school, that he finds the large group and assembly times not for him but that he is a governor and is happy to host the school during major festivals and celebrations. I can only think there are many lost opportunities to engage in the life of the school.'
- 'Ten years ago, it seemed as if schools had no place for adults—other than staff and parents—to take part in the life of the school. Now this seems entirely reversed, with a positive welcome to people from the community, including the church, to fulfil all sorts of volunteer roles.'
- 'It's about getting the whole church to say, "It's our school."'
- 'I used to see the role of a minister in school as a pied piper, being so entertaining that children would follow them into church attendance. Now, my model is of the whole church family supporting the whole school family in becoming a Christian community in its own right.'

It is clear that some ministers are not necessarily suited to leading collective worship, or being on governing boards. The school placement affords curates the opportunity to reflect upon other ways in which their presence will not only support the school, but also enhance their own personal ministry:

- 'As a local priest, I think it would be worthwhile exploring the possibility of being involved not just in "religious" things such as the assemblies/worship or RE, but actually having a Christian input into other topics as well.'
- 'Jesus goes in as a servant and says, "What can I do for you?" Why would you not? Mission of God, let's get out there!'
- 'Relationship should be non-converting—showing God's love in any way we can. Every encounter is an opportunity: after school club, spotting gifts within the parish that can be shared, laity from the church community who can help, support for staff under pressure.'

Longer-term Impact

In an effort to discover what effect the placement has had on curates in the longer term, we approached incumbents who at least two years previously had been part of the Curate School Placement programme. We hoped to find out whether the placement had indeed developed a school-shaped minister. Based on the discussions thus far, we discovered that the school placement certainly has had a positive impact on those incumbents who had been a part of the programme:

- 'I found the whole experience was very formative and proved to be one of the most memorable parts of my curacy.'
- 'My school placement was helpful because, although I had been a secondary school teacher, it had been a while since I had in-depth access to a primary school. The latest developments in the RE/values curriculum and growth mindset resources were really useful in planning what to offer the local school in my parish—as was knowing what songs were currently popular amongst that population, for service planning!'

In the first six months of taking on her incumbency the minister above had already become very involved with both schools in the parish. As well as being a governor and leading collective worship, she had run a sanctum prayer space in one school, and Easter prayer spaces for different year groups in the second school, thus shaping herself to respond to the individual needs of the schools.

Another new incumbent said:

'The placement helped me to realize what a privilege working with schools was. While I already had some sense of the fantastic opportunity to tell so many children and adults (who I would not normally meet in church) about the love of God, I had not thought about how it would deepen my own faith.

The school where I did my placement was led by a very wise, kind and faithful head who it was a blessing to encounter. I was really keen to be involved with the church school where I now work because I love them and want to help. Their willingness to let me do this is because I allow them to love and help me back, *ie* I don't act like a know-all on a pedestal.

The school contributes to my continual development as a priest.

The placement helped me to recognize the value of true relationship, which takes time and requires trust and openness on both sides, so that not only can we see Christ in the other but we learn about Christ from the other. A good chaplain learns as much as they impart, if not more!'

6 The Impact on Schools

The most dramatic impact on a school was in one with a shortfall in funding for counselling services. The curate returned to her church (a large suburban congregation), shared the need and collected £1,500 in a single week. We do not make any promises that this will ever be replicated! But we do claim that the vast majority of placements have been successful and have had an impact both on schools and curates alike (reasons for those less successful are covered in chapter four). In schools, it often makes the leaders pause and reflect on the uniqueness of their school as a church school, considering which elements of their daily life promote the Christian faith, and what more could potentially be offered:

- 'It was great to be able to share our hopes and aspirations for the school and to talk about our values and ethos with someone who was genuinely interested...and his fresh eyes were so useful to us too.'
- 'The incumbent is the bridge between [church and school] (not the pied piper for church). The school is a Christian community in its own right. Church is there to enable the school to be the best church school. God's economy—twice back in a blessing...Let God's love out and perhaps later the children will live it out.'

In other cases, merely the fact that it hosted the placement serves as a reminder that the school is a part of the larger church family:

> 'It raises the conscious awareness of what we are doing as a church school, and why.'

We also approached head teachers in parishes where their incumbents had, during curacy, undertaken a church school placement, to find out about the quality and nature of the current relationship:

> 'It has been a great privilege to work with our minister. The children have benefited greatly from his close links to our school spiritually. He has built up a very strong relationship with our children through leading collective worship, being very visual around the school...working

very closely with our school staff and has an extremely positive impact on our governing body. As well as enhancing the Christian distinctiveness of our school, he visits his link class on a regular basis and knows individual children well.'

In this particular instance, the incumbent also spoke highly of the impact that the curate placement had had on his ministry and spoke to the next cohort of curates about this, identifying clearly how he had become shaped by the school experience.

Partnership

According to another head teacher, there had been a significant change in the way that the school and church worked in partnership with each other since the incumbent, who had been a part of the School Placement Programme, had taken up post:

'She has transformed our school in the year that she has been with us, with her vibrant and refreshing outlook and attitude. Her enthusiasm for developing worship and RE is tangible but is set against a very real understanding of our school community and, as such, is appropriately judged. She has taken time to hear what staff, pupils and parents have said and this has instilled great respect and trust—and sensitivity to people's thoughts and beliefs. She attends...sessions where she might glean a sense of the culture and ethos of our school. Essentially, she has become a part of our school, rather than a "visitor."'

One school in the Diocese of Chelmsford has been involved in curate school placements from the beginning and has had a very successful and productive relationship with the incumbent. During discussions with the head teacher about strong church/school links, the head teacher told of different ways that support was given, where time allowed. This could be seen as an example of a rounded/holistic approach to working with schools—a school-shaped ministry:

The Church and the School— A Partnership of Opportunities

'How it works for us:

- She leads worship once every three weeks.
- Leads burial services for school animals that have died—chicks generally.

- Attends worship group meetings when we reflect on and plan major services in the coming term or year.
- Contributes as a governor.
- She has also led a club for those children who wish to grow in their faith.
- Is an ear, support and gentle mentor for me—helping me to avoid pitfalls…
- She takes care with her preparation every time.
- And attends school functions when she can.
- Helps to monitor the school's ethos with other staff and governors—interviewing staff and children.
- Is the link between the school and local residential homes—helping us to serve the local community through joining in services in the residential homes.
- Has baptized one of our teachers and her son.

And me?…I just welcome her and make the odd enthusiastic suggestion for how she might to get involved.'

Conclusion

Walter Brueggemann argues that the…

> …new reality turns adults towards children and children towards adults, making solidarity and well-being possible. Indeed this is the sign of the new age (see Mal 4.5–6 and Luke 1.17)…the ultimate test of readiness for the coming of the kingdom…[May we, like God (Hos 13.8)] be given the passion of a she-bear to care for every cub, our own and all the others who will not be left orphaned by the God who gives mercy to the orphans.[43]

As one curate following their placement asked,

> [Can I] be the one who has the freedom to be, to respond in the moment where necessary, to offer time, presence, acceptance…love? And to do all this without requiring anything of the over-worked, over-tested, over-analyzed, totally beloved children of God who are before us.

Through the Curate School Placement programme, schools shape ministers. In part, this shaping is about giving them the training to operate effectively in schools in future. But we believe that this shaping should go far beyond giving them skills; we believe that playful attention to the child in the midst will transform their spirituality, theology and practice, and that seeing how they engage with children will most effectively allow us to see their ministerial development in action. Schools do not just need ministers willing to be on the governing body and lead collective worship. They need people, shaped by playfulness and community and the child in the midst, becoming the sort of ministers who can love with the passion of a she-bear and be a sign of the coming of the kingdom.

Notes

1 On formation for school leaders, see A Farnell, *Grow Your Own School Leaders* (Grove Education booklet eD35).

2 H Heclo, *Thinking Institutionally* (Oxford University Press, 2008) pp 109–110.

3 A Russell, *The Clerical Profession* (London: SPCK, 1980) p 24.

4 S Collinson, *Making Disciples* (Milton Keynes: Paternoster, 2004).

5 The Church of England, *Formation Criteria for Ordained Ministry:* https://www.churchofengland.org/sites/default/files/2017-10/formation_criteria_for_ordained_ministry.pdf

6 K Vanhoozer, *Pictures at a Theological Exhibition* (London: IVP, 2016) p 184.

7 See, for example, C Brittain, 'Can a theology student be an evil genius? On the concept of *habitus* in theological education,' *Scottish Journal of Theology*, 60.4 (2007), pp 426–440.

8 See for example, A MacIntyre, *After Virtue: A Study in Moral Theory* (Notre Dame, IN: University of Notre Dame Press, 1984) and T Wright, *Virtue Reborn* (London: SPCK, 2010).

9 D Ford, *The Shape of Living* (London: Collins Fount, 1997).

10 F Ward, *Full of Character* (London: Jessica Kingsley, 2019).

11 N Morgan, *Taught not Caught* (Woodbridge: John Catt, 2017).

12 See, for example, J Taylor, 'Via Intelligentiae,' in R Heber and C P Eden (eds), *The Whole Works of the Right Rev Jeremy Taylor, DD,* Vol 8 (London: Longman, 1861) pp 359–392.

13 Our summary of the first half of 'Via Intelligentiae.'

14 Our summary of the second half of 'Via Intelligentiae,' see A Griffiths, 'How to be Good,' *ANVIL 19.3 (2002).*

15 The Church of England, *Formation Criteria for Ordained Ministry, op cit.*

16 Morgan, *op cit*, p 23.

17 Ward, *op cit*, pp 92–94.

18 J H Newman, *The Idea of a University* (New York: Longmans, Green and Co, 1899) pp 121, 134.

19 Griffiths, *op cit*, p 191.

20 Griffiths, *op cit*, p 191.

21 K Baker, *14–18: A New Vision for Secondary Education* (London: Bloomsbury, 2013).

22 McIntyre, *op cit*, p 205.

23 Personal email to the authors. A module for initial ministerial education phase 1, called 'Education for a Learning Church,' is delivered by H Worsley at Trinity College, Bristol, and by A Griffiths and others at St Mellitus College.

24 See M J Bunge (ed), *The Child in Christian Thought* (Grand Rapids, MI: Eerdmans, 2001) and M J Bunge (ed), *The Child in the Bible* (Grand Rapids, MI: Eerdmans, 2008).

25 https://www.abc.net.au/radionational/programs/spiritofthings/child-theology/4435754 [accessed 2019].

26 D Werner, *The Church and the Child* (Geneva: World Council of Churches, 2011): https://www.oikoumene.org/en/resources/documents/wcc-programmes/education-and-ecumenical-formation/ete/wcc-programme-on-ecumenical-theological-education/[accessed 2019].

27 'In a marketing culture that so openly feeds and colludes with obsession...the child as consumer is always a pseudo-adult'—R Williams, *Lost Icons* (Edinburgh: Continuum, 2000) p 23.

28 U Becker, 'The Child in Theology and Church,' *Ecumenical Review* 31 (1979), p 239.

29 Thomas Traherne, *The Way to Blessedness* (circa 1670) (London: The Faith Press, 1962) pp 106, 115.

30 Ward, *op cit*, p 123.

31 G Monbiot, *Feral: Searching for Enchantment on the Frontiers of Rewilding* (London: Allen Lane, 2013) p 9.

32 P W Goodliff, *Shaped for Service* (Eugene, OR: Pickwick, 2017) p 222.

33 K J White, 'Child Theology as Theology,' *ANVIL* 35.1 (2019) pp 13–20.

34 Matthew 18—see F Young, 'Child Theology: A theological response,' *ANVIL* 35.1 (2019) p 10.

35 Isaiah 11—see Young, *op cit*, p 10.

36 Young, *op cit*, p 8.

37 H Willmer and K J White, *Entry Point: Towards Child Theology* (London: WTL Publications, 2013). See also the two handbooks edited by M Bunge above.

38 https://www.churchofengland.org/sites/default/files/2018-04/Mental-HealthandWell-beingGuidance.pdf

39 Education is largely devolved within the UK, so this column largely refers to policy-makers for England.

40 R Nye, *Soul Searching 2: Clergy Roles in Church Schools* (Diocese of Ely, 2016).

41 *ibid.*

42 H Worsley, *Churches Linking with Schools* (Grove Education booklet eD2) p 23.

43 M J Bunge (ed), *The Child in the Bible, op cit*, p 495.